Completely
Kafka

Nicolas Mahler

Completely Kafka

Pushkin Press

Pushkin Press
Somerset House, Strand
London WC2R 1LA

Completely Kafka was first published as *Komplett Kafka* by Suhrkamp in Berlin, 2023
First published by Pushkin Press in 2024

1 3 5 7 9 8 6 4 2

ISBN 13: 978-1-80533-158-2

Typeset by Tetragon, London
Printed and bound in the United Kingdom by Elcograf S.p.A.

www.pushkinpress.com

Completely Kafka

Think of me as a dream

Over at Rabbi Löw's a light's still burning.
Though not an electric one.

It's 1852.

Rabbi Löw is a clever man, today he's making things out of clay. He fashions a creature that soon begins to grumble, cry and rage; in short: that is alive.

The creature has a name, too:
Hermann Kafka.

Hermann is always in a bad mood, his language coarse. He has
a *penchant for rude phrases, uttered as loudly as possible*; he
refers to the rabbi's good cooking as *grub* and *cleans his ears
with toothpicks.* The only thing that's important to him is that
one *cuts bread straight.* Not an easy guy.

The rabbi soon finds this too much to bear and bans his creature from the house.

But Hermann goes his own way. He's tenacious, he has a *great entrepreneurial spirit* and finds a wife who is devoted to him, who toils away in his shop and at home: Julie Kafka, née Löwy.

Thirty-one years later.

Rabbi Löw lives alone, he even keeps house himself. He comes across a sad, dried-out little lump of clay beneath the bed.

The rabbi is really touched; he's always had a hard time throwing things away.

And so the rabbi stops what he's doing and goes back to his alchemical work.

There's not a lot to it, but if you stretch it out enough, it becomes a rather charming little figure.

Ach, Rabbi, if only you hadn't given life to the sad little lump of clay.
How much anxiety, pain and procrastination the little creature would have been spared.

Is there anything to this backstory?
Probably not, Rabbi Löw died in 1609, in Prague.
And Franz Kafka doesn't have much to do with Judaism.

Hermann Kafka only *goes to temple four times a year*, and later on Franz will write: *And I yawned and I dozed throughout the long hours (as far as boredom goes, the temple was only ever matched by dance lessons).*

From an early age, Franz has suffered from countless fears, he is terribly afraid of mirrors because *they showed me in what I consider to be my unavoidable ugliness, which, moreover, couldn't have been completely true, for if I had really looked like that, I surely would have attracted more attention.*

You can't achieve anything with this kind of body,

I shall have to get used to its continuous failings.

The coarse father and his sensitive son, *that anxious and small bundle of bones*, are a curious team. *After all, your sheer physical presence already weighed me down*, Kafka writes years later in his *Letter to His Father*.

I remember, for example, how we would often undress together in the same changing room. Me: skinny, slight, feeble; you: strong, tall, broad. Even in the changing room I felt pitiful, and what's more, not only in your eyes, but in those of the entire world, because for me you were the standard by which everything was measured.

His father is not only physically overpowering but extraordinarily stubborn to boot.

For Hermann, only one opinion counts: his own. He is always right, everyone else is

You were capable, for instance, of disparaging the Czechs, and then the Germans, and then the Jews, and what's more, not just partially but in every respect, until, ultimately, nobody was left but you.

Kafka's *Letter to His Father* will become a fixture of world literature, but the addressee, of all people, never read it.

Maybe the massive letter was simply too long—after all, it contains over one hundred handwritten pages.

Hermann Kafka is not a reader.

Next to his scary father, *in the confusion of childhood* his mother appears *as the archetype of reason.*
Julie Kafka is full of understanding and affection, but her son soon realizes that she's mistaken about him.

She takes me for a healthy young man, who simply suffers from a bit of hypochondria.

Another big problem: how to dress.

I noticed, of course, which was rather easy, that I was particularly poorly dressed, but I also had an eye for when others were well dressed, and yet for years my mind couldn't manage to find the cause of my miserable appearance in my clothes.

And then there are his three sisters, too.

Kafka describes the eldest, Elli, as a *clumsy, tired, timid, bad-tempered, guilt-ridden, overly shy, spiteful, lazy, greedy, miserly child, I could hardly bring myself to look at her, much less speak to her, that's how much she reminded me of myself... I found her miserliness especially abhorrent, as I had it, if possible, to an even greater extent.*

In the second, Valli, Franz sees few *Kafkaesque traits.*

The youngest, Ottla, comes off best. She is considered Kafka's favourite.

For their father, on the other hand, she is *a kind of devil.*

You yourself have confessed to me that, in your opinion, she is always making you suffer and annoying you on purpose, and that your suffering on her account satisfies and pleases her.

Youth's meaninglessness. Fear of youth, fear of meaninglessness, of the meaningless rise of an inhuman life, this is Kafka's youth.

Not to mention his *fear of school*. And yet, despite it all, he manages to make it through the difficult German Gymnasium.

He only achieves this feat, however, *by crying during examinations*, especially maths.

His horrible school days are now behind him, but what is to come is no less unpleasant.

Since I always considered my inability to be my only path into the future... pondering the future never did me any good, it was only a spinning-out of my present grief.

Kafka suffers from a sense of *earthly weight*.
And yet, every now and then, there are flashes of hope.

Of course there are
possibilities for me,
but beneath which stone?

He is never light-hearted. Wherever he is, there is always a reason to brood.

Everything immediately gives me pause. Every joke in the comic paper, what I remember about Flaubert and Grillparzer, the sight of my parents' nightshirts laid out on their bed for the night...

I stand on the end platform of the tram and am completely unsure of my footing in this world, in this town, in my family.

From his mid-twenties on, Kafka, law degree under his belt, works for various insurance companies.
Among other things, there he devotes himself to *measures for preventing accidents from wood-planing machines.*

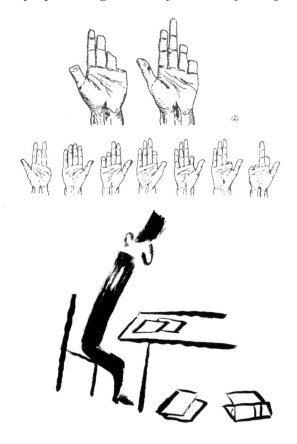

In the office now. I am at the Assicurazioni-Generali but have hopes of one day sitting in chairs in faraway countries, looking out of the office windows at fields of sugar cane or Mohammedan cemeteries; and though the whole world of insurance itself interests me greatly, my present work is dreary. Adieu.

After work he exchanges one desk for another. At home
in his room, he plunges into his own texts.
I shall jump into my novella even if it cuts my face to pieces.
But, hemmed in between his parents'
bedroom and the living room,
there is no peace to be found.

*I want to write, with a constant trembling on my forehead. I sit
in my room in the very headquarters of the uproar of the entire
house. I can hear each and every door close and it is only thanks
to the noise that I am spared the sound of the footsteps of those
running between them, I can even hear the slam of the oven
door in the kitchen. My father bursts into my room and passes
through, his dressing gown dragging behind him; someone
scrapes the ashes out of the stove next door.*

Deep *in the dregs of misery* he doesn't feel any better either.

That is how Kafka later describes his office at the *Workers' Accident Insurance Institute for the Kingdom of Bohemia.*

I know only what lies on top, and that casually;
below I can only suspect terrible things.

Kafka finds his existence to be a kind of *horrible double life, from which there is probably no escape but insanity.*

In a letter he sums things up: *Time is short, my strength limited, the office a horror, the apartment noisy.*

And yet, outwardly Kafka appears normal.

The author and critic Max Brod writes: 'At first glance, Kafka was a healthy young man, if strangely quiet, observing, reserved.'

In fact, Kafka was a handsome figure, over one metre eighty centimetres tall, that is, more than ten centimetres taller than the average Czech at that time.

Visually speaking, Brod is the opposite.
He is short, with a somewhat strange posture, the curvature of his spine forcing him to wear a *back straightener*, a frame made of metal bars.

Nevertheless (or as a result?), Brod is far more successful with women than Kafka is.

Contrary to the usual clichés, the *straightened-out* Brod describes Kafka as a healthy, *natural-healer type*.

'Intellectually, he was by no means attracted to the interesting-sickly, the bizarre, the grotesque, but towards the greatness of nature, towards what healed, the salutary, the healthily solid, the simple... and those who see Kafka as something of a desert monk and anchorite are completely mistaken.'

Nor should we forget that he practised *gymnastics naked in front of an open window for ten minutes a day.*

'I admired Franz's swimming and rowing skills, especially the way he handled a so-called "soul-drinker".'

Kafka's diaries, however, give a different impression:

I work with weights I cannot get rid of.

Total block. Endless torments.

Whatever I touch comes apart.

I don't hide from people because I want to live quietly, but because I want to expire quietly.

Day before yesterday criticized over the factory.
Then an hour on the sofa considering jumping out of the window.

And yet he has a strong *need for pleasure.*
He likes to go to the movies with his friend Brod.

Kafka meticulously records his viewing experiences in his diary:
Was at the movies. Cried. Lolotte. *The good minister. The little bicycle. The parents' reconciliation. Tremendously entertained. Before it the sad* The Accident on the Dock, *after it the gay* Alone at Last.
His conclusion:
I am capable of enjoying human relationships, but not experiencing them.

Together with Brod, Kafka forges commercially motivated plans, too. His dream: a series of bestsellers. Brod reports:

'We had the idea of creating a new type of travel guide. It was to be called *CHEAP*... So, *Cheap through Switzerland, Cheap in Paris,* and so on.'

'Franz was indefatigable and took a childish delight in expanding the principles of this type, which was to make us millionaires and, above all, to rescue us from our dreadful office jobs, down to the last detail. A special joke of ours concerned a *Cheap* phrase book which was to be based on the principle that it is impossible to learn a foreign language completely. Our idea, then, was that we go ahead and teach the wrong language straight away.'

Their friends *have a good laugh* about such ideas.

But the *Cheap* volumes never appear, nothing comes of their *multimillion-dollar* idea. The idea is just *too* good.

Brod: 'I then also seriously corresponded with publishers about our plans for *travel guide reform*. But negotiations failed as we did not want to divulge the precious secret without a huge advance.'

Now, over a hundred years later, the secret can be revealed:

CHEAP will save the traveller from having to choose, CHEAP contains only imperative routes, just ONE hotel per city, just ONE mode of transportation, the cheapest.

CHEAP
1. ~~~~

Kafka is very disappointed about *Cheap*'s failure to happen, even if later on Brod admits: 'Often it was hard to tell whether he meant something seriously or whether he was joking. Franz was particularly fond of straddling the line between seriousness and jest and did so with a high degree of virtuosity.'

And so the *Cheap* series never appears; in its place, however, is a volume by the name of *Contemplation*. A book of conspicuously small size, as Kafka neatly *tidies up the pieces* while in the process of arranging them. He considered only a few of his early stories to be ready for print.

Out,
out,
out

There's a worm here
somewhere that can
even hollow out
this story's plenitude,

Due to the *improbably small selection*, Kafka asks the publishers for *the largest font size possible, within those intentions that you have for the book.*

The request is granted.
'With their giant letters the ninety-nine pages of the first edition resemble ancient votive tablets,' Brod observes sheepishly.

Kafka is rather severe when it comes to women, too.

Agathe is very ugly and so is Hedwig. H. is small and fat, her cheeks an uninterrupted red and boundless, her upper front teeth are large and that makes it impossible for the mouth to close and her lower jaw to be small; she is very short-sighted, and not only because of the pretty movement with which she sets her pince-nez down on her nose—the tip of which is really beautifully composed of small planes; tonight I dreamt of her short, thick legs, and it is thanks to these detours that I recognize a girl's beauty and fall in love.

But then Kafka meets Felice Bauer and everything changes. Or maybe not.

In his diary he records their first encounter:

Frl. Felice Bauer. When I came to Brod on 13th August, she was sitting at the table and, to me, looked like a maid. Nor was I at all curious about who she was, I simply accepted her presence. A bony, empty face that wore its emptiness openly. Bare neck. Breezily worn blouse. An almost broken nose, blonde, somewhat stiff, charmless hair, strong chin. As I sat down, I looked at her more closely for the first time, and by the time I was in my chair had already formed an unshakable judgement.

Two years later the following:

The argumentation in general: I am lost to F.

A month after their first meeting he writes, as if intoxicated, 'The Judgement' in a single night.

Kafka, the serious author, is born. Even he is satisfied with the story.
In a letter to the publisher Kurt Wolff, Kafka describes this father–son story as *my favourite work*.

The critic of the *Dürerbund Literary Annual* sees things differently. For him 'The Judgement' is a 'painstakingly inflated mental-health study'.

Kafka keeps a careful eye on his reviews.

Soon the word the critics employ most often is: *bizarre.*
He finds sympathetic reviews to be nothing but *lavish praise*, considers them to be based on *misunderstanding* and particularly *useless* when written by acquaintances (like his friend Brod).

He finds negative reviews, however, to be:

reasonable.

In any case, Kafka would have preferred to see the greater part of his oeuvre destroyed.

Of all that I have written only the following books count: 'The Judgement', 'The Stoker', The Metamorphosis, 'In the Penal Colony', 'A Country Doctor' and the story 'A Hunger Artist'.
Everything else will be published posthumously against his wishes, thanks to the actions of Max Brod.

Kafka's works are among the most interpreted in literary history.
But what do they really mean?
Sometimes Kafka himself isn't all that sure.

Can you discern any kind of sense in THE JUDGEMENT? I can't, and I can't explain a thing in it either!

In one of his countless letters to Felice he continues:
'The Judgement' cannot be explained. Perhaps one day I'll show you some diary entries about it. The story is full of abstractions, though they are never admitted. The friend doesn't really exist, perhaps he is more whatever the father and Georg have in common. The story may be a journey around father and son, and the friend's changing shape may be a change in perspective in the father and son's relationship. But I'm not really all that sure about this either.

Perhaps Kafka is just flirting.
He is a lot more direct to his friend Brod:

A year after 'The Judgement' Kafka writes a story that will send shivers down the spines of generations of schoolkids to come: *The Metamorphosis*.

As Gregor Samsa awoke one morning from uneasy dreams, he found that he had been transformed into a monstruous bug.

Kafka, who likes to draw, has severe apprehensions about the cover design for *The Metamorphosis*. He rightly suspects that the commissioned illustrator might be planning to draw the beetle.

The beetle itself cannot be drawn.
It cannot be shown even from afar, Kafka writes to his publisher, Kurt Wolff.

Would Kafka agree with the *following* representation of Gregor transformed into a bug?

While Gregor rails against having to get up early and his new appearance, his family outside the door begin to grow anxious.

The recently hatched bug tries to put off its tedious relatives.

To stand up he would have needed arms and hands—instead, all he had were those many little constantly moving legs, over which, moreover, he had no control.

Just the thing to read at school.
Indeed, what schoolkid isn't familiar with this little morning issue?

In the end, the terrible *metamorphosis* is impossible to keep a secret any longer.

Only the cleaning woman, an *old widow who, in her long life, has already survived the worst thanks to her strong bone structure*, takes Gregor's new form in her stride.

Eventually Gregor manages to control his newly acquired legs to *criss-cross the walls and ceiling* and ends up hanging off the latter, now and again *dropping to the floor with a smack.*

In the interim, due to financial reasons, one of his parents' rooms has been let to three bearded lodgers, who are *rather particular about order.*

Gregor, who is now confidently scuttling about, disturbs the three lodgers' sense of hygiene.

They give notice to leave *immediately*.

The lodgers are gone, and Gregor won't be around for much longer either.

The apple-pelting scene comes now!

Gregor never recovers from his father's action. The apple remains *embedded in his flesh*, it begins to rot, the beetle dies.

For all the comedy, *The Metamorphosis* ends tragically. It's not just the tough cleaning woman who shows little compassion; Gregor's family are relieved, too.

In the end, the family take a tram ride. The daughter develops magnificently; the son is dead.

Interlude
KAFKA'S PRESS REVIEWS

'Fr. Kafka tells in a rather colourless way the grotesque story of a salesman who wakes up one morning as a crustacean, frightens his family, is fed by them for a while, and ultimately dies. This *Metamorphosis* is told with calm and skill, but in a rather unimaginative and boring way.'
Dürerbund Literary Annual

'This book is all one big father-problem. It is the old lament of a son who cannot cope with his parents, a son who suffers bitterly from himself and his family and for whom all these pains are now condensed into a bug fantasy.'
Prager Tagblatt

The critics aren't the only ones who are perplexed. Several months after the appearance of *The Metamorphosis* Kafka receives the following letter:

Dear Sir,

You have made me unhappy. I bought your Metamorphosis *and gave it to my cousin. But she does not have the faintest idea of how to explain the story. She gave it to her mother, who does not know how to explain it either.*

My mother gave the book to my other cousin, and she does not know how to explain it. Now they have written to me. They want me to explain the story to them. As I am the doctor in the family. But I am at a loss, sir!

I spent months in the trenches fighting the Russians and did not bat an eyelid. But were my reputation with my cousins to go to hell, I could not bear it. Only you can help me. You must, as you are the one who got me into this mess.

So do please tell me what my cousins should think about The Metamorphosis.

Respectfully yours,
Dr Siegfried Wolff

No reply of Kafka's has come down to us.

Despite all the criticism, *The Metamorphosis* generates enough of a buzz to inspire an unauthorized continuation.

It is written by the twenty-year-old Karl Brand, an admirer of Kafka.

The 'Re-Metamorphosis of Gregor Samsa' appears in the *Prager Tagblatt* half a year after Kafka's text.

In Brand's story the seemingly dead beetle awakes upon a pile of dung and begins to turn back into Gregor Samsa.

He was horrified to find that he had fingers, human hands.

Following a laborious transformation, Gregor once again learns how to walk and steps off the dung heap into a positive future.
The story ends with the line:
A new life begins!

The author himself has no hope of a miraculous recovery.

At the time of 'Re-Metamorphosis' Karl Brand has already
suffered for years from tuberculosis and cannot work.
In another one of his unpublished works he writes:

*I lie there or crawl about, like a bedbug or a dung beetle, not fit
for a thing.*

Nine months after the appearance of his text Brand dies,
impoverished, in his family's apartment in Prague.

While his unknown double was on his deathbed, Kafka continued to write letters to his eternal fiancée Felice. What kind of woman wouldn't have been charmed by the following?

I am not doing well, what with all the effort I need to keep myself alive and sane I could have built the pyramids. Franz

Hundreds of letters are sent, actual encounters are rare. And this despite Kafka's later writing:

All the unhappiness of my life comes from letters, or the possibility of writing letters. You know how much I hate letters. Written kisses do not arrive but are drunk up along the way by ghosts.

When Felice doesn't reply immediately, Kafka threatens to lose it:

20th November 1912: Dearest, what have I done to you for you to torture me so? No letter from you today either, not with the first, not with the second post.

21st November 1912: Dearest! Poor child! You have a miserable and utterly uncomfortable lover. When he doesn't receive a letter from you for two days, he lashes out senselessly, even if only with words.

14th April 1913: Telegram
yet again no news please please a frank word

25th May 1913: For God's sake, why aren't you writing me? No word for a whole week. This is horrible indeed.

But his letter-writing compulsion is increasingly getting on his own nerves.

I am overcome with disgust, Felice, when I think of you on a lovely morning, for the most part well rested, looking forward to a pleasant day, sitting down for breakfast while day after day my damn letters arrive like messages from the land of the dead.

But what should I do, Felice?

Do letters like this make it better?

How can Felice take it?
Kafka has other, brighter sides too.

I can laugh too, Felice, believe it or not.

I'm even known as a hearty laugher.

Max Brod confirms as much, but specifies:
'Of course, it was not an entirely convivial, comforting laugh.
But there was an element of convivial laughter there.'

Kafka corresponds not only with Felice, but also with their mutual friend Grete Bloch.
Here Kafka shows himself to be a little less than gallant and has a few words regarding Felice's teeth.

At the beginning, to be honest, I had to lower my eyes whenever I saw F.'s teeth, all that flashy gold (in that inappropriate place a really hellish shine) and yellow-grey porcelain. Later, when I could, I'd look at them on purpose, so as not to forget it, to torture myself and, ultimately, convince myself that it was really true.

Despite her *hellacious* teeth, Kafka is crazy about photos of Felice. He literally begs her for them.

I realize that this would be, of course, the most inappropriate time to beg you to give or lend me a photograph. I am aware of that.

But when she sends him a *little pic*, once again he is unhappy.

A lovely picture, it's just that you look happier in others. And your collar spoils it, too. If I'm not mistaken, Mephisto wears a collar like that, I've seen Strindberg with one too, but you, Felice?

He isn't all that sure about the engagement anyway, the prospect of marriage frightens him.

I am greedy for solitude, the idea of a honeymoon appals me, the sight of any newlyweds, whether I know them or not, fills me with disgust, and if I want to make myself ill, all I have to do is imagine putting my arm round some woman's hips.

Again and again he attempts to end the relationship.

Quickly forget the spectre that I am and go on living happily and quietly as before.

In any event, Kafka's primary interest remains writing.

I hate everything that has nothing to do with literature, having conversations (even when they have to do with literature) bores me, paying visits bores me, my relatives' sorrows and joys bore me to the depths of my soul.

He flees for Golden Lane, also known as the Street of the Alchemists. His sister Ottla has a tiny house there, where he can find the quiet to work.

But he remains unhappy with it; writing (once again) to Felice, he says:

Poor, poor dear, please never feel forced into reading this miserable novel I am putting together in such a lacklustre manner.

The *miserable novel, The Man Who Disappeared*, also remains unfinished. In Kafka's lifetime only the first chapter, 'The Stoker', is published.

Max Brod observes: 'While writing his novella "The Stoker", which took place in America, he didn't want to hear a thing about America even though he had never been there. He wrote the America of his head and heart, one in which the Statue of Liberty doesn't carry a torch but a sword, as it fitted the sentence better.'

Why does the novel take place in America at all? The reason: the sixteen-year-old Karl Roßmann escapes there after fathering a child in a rather *uncomfortable* situation with the considerably older servant girl, Fräulein Brummer.

And what was Fräulein Brummer like?

Sometimes she would kneel down in her little room off the kitchen and pray to a wooden cross. Sometimes she would scamper about the kitchen before retreating, laughing like a witch whenever she and Karl crossed paths.

No wonder Karl skipped out on Fräulein Brummer and their child and took a ship on the Hamburg–America line.

But immediately upon his arrival in America everything goes wrong. First he forgets his umbrella in the hull, then he manages to lose his suitcase.

A bit later he meets two men with wonderful names, Mr Schubal and Mr Pollunder, but women remain a difficulty. The first one he encounters in America, Fräulein Klara, wants to throw him right out of the window.

The defenestration isn't exactly successful, but Klara still intends to *smack Karl about a bit*, until his *cheeks swell*.

Karl takes it all in stride, he is driven by something else: *What he really needed to do was stretch out and yawn.*

Of course, just lying around won't work. Karl's got to make some money.

At the Hotel Occidental the head chef, Grete Mitzelbach of Vienna, takes him under her wing.

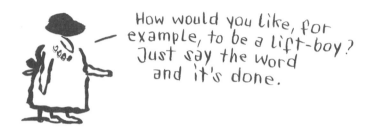

How would you like, for example, to be a lift-boy? Just say the word and it's done.

Karl receives a lovely *lift-boy uniform with gold buttons and braid.*

But:

Especially under the arms the short jacket was cold, stiff and, thanks to the sweat of the lift-boys who'd worn it before him, impossible to dry.

But Karl doesn't keep the cold little jacket on for long; soon we find him naked in bed, this time beset by the typist Therese, from Pomerania.

Following this jolt, Karl relocates to a dorm room overflowing with lift-boys busy beating one another with abandon.

But Karl's career as a lift-boy doesn't last long.

His dubious acquaintance, Robinson, has a vomiting fit in the hotel foyer and this puts an end to his employment.

Not even head chef Grete Mitzelbach can help; Karl is fired on the spot.

Thereafter Karl gets beaten black and blue by head porter Feodor,

fondled by the opera singer Brunelda's *fat little hand...*

and, in the midst of *a crazy jumble of furniture*, thrown against a wardrobe by Brunelda's French lover.

As nothing seems to be working out, Karl joins the theatre.

Getting into the *Nature Theatre of Oklahoma* isn't all that tough, they simply accept *everyone*.

Having said that, the welcome committee is rather peculiar.

It was a confused mess, the trumpets weren't in tune with one another, they all just blew on to their hearts' content.

The *Nature Theatre of Oklahoma* may be *the biggest theatre in the world*, but no one seems to have ever seen it. Just what it has to do with nature theatre remains an open question.

Moreover, it was difficult to understand anything amid the trumpets' noise.

And, to top things off, it's far away indeed, in Oklahoma. And that's where Karl needs to go.

The Man Who Disappeared remains a fragment, and things with Felice don't progress any further either. Incapable of making any decision, the dithering Kafka finally turns to Felice's father, Herr Carl Bauer:

Dear Herr Bauer!
You know your daughter, she is a fun, healthy, confident girl who needs to have fun, healthy, vibrant people around her to live. You only know me from my visits (I almost want to say it should be enough). I am taciturn, unsociable, sullen, selfish, hypochondriac, and in fact sickly. Over the last few years I have spoken on average twenty words a day with my mother and have hardly ever exchanged more than a few words of greeting with my father. I don't speak to my married sisters and brothers-in-law at all unless I am angry with them. I lack any living sense of family. And your daughter, whose nature, as that of a healthy girl, has predestined her for real marital bliss, is supposed to live next to such a person? Now there are three of us, you be the judge! Yours sincerely, Dr F. Kafka

Kafka does not make the decision easy for him.

That same year this son-in-law-in-the-making writes one of his most brutal stories, 'In the Penal Colony'. It will only be published years later and will solidify Kafka's reputation as a writer who shocks.

Writing in the *Weltbühne*, Kurt Tucholsky (under the pseudonym of Peter Panter) gives a snappy summary:

'The story is simple: in the penal colony a rebellious solider is bound to a crazy machine, and tortured. There his sentence—*respect your superiors*—is written into his naked flesh. With needles.'

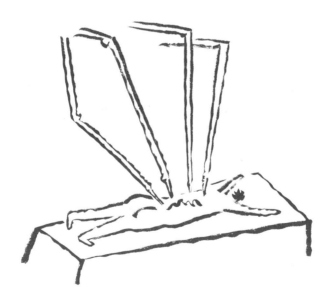

'In the Penal Colony' does not impress the critics whatsoever.

Interlude

'F. Kafka describes a torture apparatus and the pathological love of its inventor for the same, probably intended to be a psychol. study, one does not really know, as the book is too boring to stimulate deeper thought and empathy.'

Dürerbund Literary Annual

'The nastiness of the human animal, which enjoys and revels in such torment, reported as a matter of course, can only generate disgust.'

The Journal for Booklovers

Kafka rarely gives public readings, but seems to enjoy them, as he recounts to Felice in a letter:

Dearest, I just love to read out loud like hell, roaring into the audience's prepared and attentive ears does the poor heart so much good.

Speaking of hell, the reviewer from the *Münchener Zeitung* finds reading 'In the Penal Colony' hellish:

'When it comes to horror, Kafka is a true debauchee. He doesn't even shy away from the disgusting and revolting—here is no doubt that a limit has been reached, and for my taste and my nerves even partially exceeded.'

The eye-witness Max Pulver seems to recall: 'A dull thud, confusion in the hall, an unconscious woman is carried out. Two more times his words strike people unconscious. The rows of listeners begin to thin out. Some manage to flee right before being overcome by the poet's vision.'

Max Brod later: 'Not a word of that is true.'

During this phase yet another novel remains unfinished: *The Trial.*

Someone must have been badmouthing Josef K., for without having done anything wrong, one morning he was arrested.

Nor will he ever learn of *what* he has been accused.

Later K. will see the two men again, but this time without any trousers.

In a storage room K. becomes a witness to a strange scene.

While *The Trial* is considered a dark novel, Kafka himself found it so funny that, intending to read the first chapter aloud to Max Brod, he laughed so hard that 'for a while, it was impossible for him to read any further,' Brod states.

At the end of *The Trial,* two other *pale and fat* men appear and stab K. to death with a butcher's knife.

Perhaps not the best payoff, but nevertheless in some way a happy ending; Kafka once noted in his diary:

Early this morning for the first time in a long while the joy of imagining a knife driven into my heart.

He finds *the other trial*, the one he says he is subjected to at the *Askanischer Hof* hotel on 12th July 1914, decidedly less amusing. After hundreds of Kafkaesque letters and procrastinations, Felice finally cracks. We can only speculate what led her to it.

Perhaps Grete Bloch blurted out something about their letters?

The engagement is terminated. But life goes on.
Three weeks later Kafka notes in his diary:

Germany has declared war on Russia.
– In the afternoon, swimming lessons.

Following the brutal split there are further encounters with Felice, but both remain stubborn.

There is no discussion as regards my demand for a life full of fantasy, calculated only in terms of my work; deaf to all silent requests, she wants mediocrity, the comfortable flat, interest in the factory, abundant food, sleep from 11 p.m., a heated room.

Coming together would be nice, but, in the end, it is not for us...

ultimately, you are indeed a girl and want a man and not a limp worm on the ground.

... in other words, there is no future.

The struggle with Felice lasts five years. When the two, after a lot of back-and-forth, risk an engagement once more, even Max Brod can no longer look on.

'Comically enough, the two paid me a formal visit, too, the sight of these two somewhat bashful people, especially little Franz in his uncomfortable, high collar, had something touching to it, and ghastly at the same time.'

A serious haemorrhage spells the sudden end of any marriage plans.

The gushing from my throat lasted ten minutes or more, I thought it might never end.

Kafka now has a new partner, his illness.

Brod notes in his diary:
'Measures against Kafka's illness. He portrays them as psychic in nature, as an escape from marriage, as it were. He calls it: his irrevocable defeat! And yet he has slept well ever since. Freed?—Tortured soul!'

In fact, Kafka seems to be in a better mood than over the previous months.

Dear Max, my illness? Truth be told I hardly notice it. I have come to think that tuberculosis, in the form I have it, is no real illness, no real illness worthy of the name, but only a reinforcement of the general death-seed. In three weeks I've gained 2.5 kilos, which is to say, made the carrying-off that much more difficult.

His fear of the honeymoon was worse.

Kafka attempts to convalesce in a Bohemian village.

There a young woman runs across his path, another future fiancée: Julie Wohryzek. In a letter to Brod he describes her as *a young girl, hopefully only a little ill, in love with the cinema, operettas, and comedy, powder and whisky. Possessor of an inexhaustible and unstoppable supply of the cheekiest slang, on the whole very ignorant, more funny than sad—that's more or less who she is. And yet, at heart, she is brave, honest, absent-minded—such great qualities in a creature who is certainly not without physical beauty, but as insignificant as the gnat flying against the light of my lamp.*

There won't be any marriage to her, either; he abandons her. Albeit with a guilty conscience, of course.

Kafka's vampire novel, *The Castle*, takes place in a Czech village too. But watch out! Typical Kafka: there is no vampire in it at all. The uncanny thing in Kafka here is the castle itself. Kafka's protagonist, the *supposed* land surveyor K., never sets foot in Count Westwest's castle.

The village, with its mistrustful inhabitants, bizarre officials and annoying teachers, is already creepy enough for K.

You have, Herr Land Surveyor, to clean and heat both classrooms daily, as well as take care of little repairs in the building, and the school and gymnastics equipment, keep the path through the garden free of snow, run errands for me and the Fräulein Teacher, and, in the warmer months keep up with all the gardening.

In short, as we said, a horror story.

F.W. Murnau's classic vampire film *Nosferatu: A Symphony of Horror* appears at almost the same time as Kafka's novel. The similarities are striking.

Count Orlok, the vampire, lives, like Kafka's Count Westwest, in a castle. But Orlok can't stand it there any longer and would rather move to the city, to *a beautiful, dilapidated home.*

Kafka, too, is still dissatisfied with his *Castle*; the text remains a fragment.

Whether Kafka, the film buff, ever saw *Nosferatu* remains unknown.

In the meantime Kafka has struck up an epistolary relationship with the translator Milena Jesenská. Unlike Julie Wohryzek, for him Milena is no gnat but *a vigorous fire, unlike any I have ever seen*, as he writes to Brod.

Unfortunately, Milena's fire burns not for Kafka but for Ernst Polak, her husband, a lanky literary man, if one without any works to his name.

In this particular case, the gnat is Kafka. Milena is not prepared to leave her husband.

In one of his numerous letters to Milena, Kafka complains that *we are both married, you in Vienna, I to my angst in Prague, and that not only you but I as well pull in vain at our marriage.*

Milena translates a few of Kafka's stories into Czech and publishes feuilletons in the Prague newspaper *Tribuna*.

'I can still see how eagerly Kafka would run to a newspaper stand to look if the latest edition had something by Milena in it,' Brod reports.

Kafka is smitten with Milena, but there are several arguments against any relationship, and not simply the one of her being married: Kafka hates Vienna, Milena lives there.

I do not want (Milena, help me! Please understand more than I say!!!), I do not want (this isn't a stutter) to come to Vienna, as, mentally speaking, I simply would not be able to handle it. I am mentally ill, my pulmonary disease is simply an outgrowth of my mental disease.

Nevertheless, Kafka gives it his best epistolary shot.
By his standards, his courting here comes off pretty well.

I am dirty, Milena, endlessly dirty, that is why I make such a fuss about purity. No one sings as purely as those who are in the deepest hell: what we believe to be the songs of the angels are really theirs.

He also makes a go of depicting his exciting day-to-day.

Perhaps I should tell you a bit more about the evening, I was tired, empty, bored, beatable, apathetic, and from the outset wanted nothing but my bed.

Milena and Kafka's correspondence has become famous worldwide. But what exactly is it all about? Milena's letters have not survived, only Kafka's have. In one of his many letters he gives a summary:

And anyway we keep on writing the same thing. Once I ask if you are sick and then you write about it, once I want to die and then you do, once I want stamps and then you do, once I want to cry in front of you like a little boy and then you in front of me like a little girl. And once and again and a thousand times and evermore I want to be with you and you say so, too. Enough. Enough.

It's hopeless anyhow.
And these letters are nothing but torture, they begin in incurable torment, cause only incurable torment, what's the point—

And so once again he manages to avoid landing in the port of marriage he so dreads; all the same, in 1920 he does manage to make it into the *GREAT BESTIARY OF MODERN LITERATURE.*

Franz Blei analyses therein the output of contemporary authors in the style of a zoological treatise.

On Kafka we find the following entry:

The Kafka. The Kafka is a very rarely seen, magnificent and moon-blue-coloured mouse, which eats no meat but lives on bitter herbs. Its glance is fascinating, for it has human eyes.

Kafka's next protagonist doesn't even feed on *bitter herbs*, he eats nothing at all.

He is *A Hunger Artist*.

This is the tale of a kind of vaudeville act going hungry in his cage, which is watched over round the clock.

The warders, there to prevent the hunger artist from eating, are mere accessories. The hunger artist would never cheat. *The honour of his art forbade it.*

He alone knew how easy it was to go hungry. It was the easiest thing in the world.

In any event, the performance goes smoothly, for a time thousands of pleasure seekers stream to the hunger artist's cage.

Just try explaining the art of hunger to someone!
It is impossible to make it at all comprehensible to those who do not feel it.

Then, however, his fasting shows fall out of fashion.
The hunger artist becomes passé.

But:
What was the hunger artist to do? The hunger artist was not too
old to take up another occupation, he was just too fanatically
devoted to starving.

And so the hunger artist goes on practising, ignored by both audience and warders.

Shortly before his death, we even learn, rather atypically for Kafka, the reason for his fasting (warning: spoiler!).

Because I couldn't
find the food
I liked,

Kafka has already ceased to work at the *Workers' Accident Insurance Institute*. He had made it to the position of *Senior Secretary*.
And now?

Walks, nights, days, unfit for anything but pain.

Kafka is marked by his illness but has enough strength for one last story. It has to do with a rodent.

Josephine is a popular singer among the mouse people.
Although: that's not entirely true.

Is it even a song at all? Is it not perhaps only a kind of whistling?
In any event, we are all familiar with whistling, it is the artistry
of our people, or rather, not proficiency but a characteristic
expression of life. We all whistle, but admittedly no one would
think to call it art.

Nevertheless, Josephine exerts a great fascination over the mouse people. But the reason why remains a mystery.

Josephine remains firm, this nothing of a voice, this nothing of a performance remains firm and in so doing creates a path to us, it is something well worth reflecting upon.
A true singer, were one to be found among us, would be unbearable to us in times like these and we would unanimously dismiss the senselessness of just such a performance.

Only a few of the mouse people are sceptical.

She can't even whistle, she's got to make such a terrible effort just to force our customary whistle out of herself to some degree at all.

Josephine punishes her critics with nothing but *a cocky, haughty smile*, she develops into an aloof diva.

Josephine feels it befits her fame *that, with regard for her singing, she should be free from any kind of work; that is to say, any anxiety as regards her daily bread and anything and everything connected to our struggle for survival should be taken care of by someone else.*

The mouse people, however, draw other conclusions.

Josephine's request is unanimously rejected; she has crossed the line.

This people, so easily moved, sometimes cannot be moved at all.

Thereafter things go downhill for Josephine.

Soon the time will come when her last whistle shall sound and go silent.
She is but a tiny episode in the eternal history of our people and our people will get over the loss. Perhaps we will not miss her much at all, but she, delivered from the earth's woes, will happily lose herself in the countless multitude of our heroes, and soon enough, as we are not historians, be forgotten in a heightened state of redemption, along with all her brothers and sisters.

After writing down Josephine's fate, Kafka notices: something isn't right with his throat.

On 10th April 1923 Max Brod notes in his diary: 'Laryngeal tuberculosis identified. The most terrible ill-starred day.'

Kafka loses weight, his doctors prescribe a *silence cure* to protect his throat.
His larynx is closing.

Soon eating and speaking become virtually impossible, so Kafka begins to write down key words and demands on little slips of paper.

One of these *conversation cards* says:

The story has a new title:
Josephine the Singer, or the Mouse People.

Rather late in the proceedings a new partner enters the stage: Dora Diamant.

She accompanies Kafka on his last, hopeless trip through three sanatoriums. He wants to marry her, but again something gets in the way.

'Dora's care for the sick man was touching, as was the late awakening of all his vital energies,' Brod writes. 'And now, *in articulo mortis*, he would have known how to live and lived willingly.'

At the end, irrecoverably lost to tuberculosis, he manages to correct his final proofs.
Eerily enough, of all things they are those of 'A Hunger Artist'.

He is not unhappy with the story, he finds it:

Bearable.

At this point in time Kafka could no longer eat.

Concerning the dying man Brod reports:
'He wanted people to take long drinks of water (or beer) in front of him, something that was impossible for him to do; he found joy in others' pleasure. Over his last days he spoke a lot about drinks and fruit.'

Have you already tasted last year's wine, Doctor?

Brod is impressed by how stoically his friend bears his pain. The only complaint of Kafka's he recalls is that *there are so many stations on the way to your death, it goes so slowly*!

It takes so long for you to be packed down and stuffed through this one final, narrow hole.

On Tuesday, 3rd June 1924, Franz Kafka dies. He is forty.

Many of the important women in Kafka's life fall victim to the Nazis.

All of his sisters die in the gas chambers, Elli and Valli in Chelmno, Ottla in Auschwitz.

Julie Wohryzek and Grete Bloch are murdered in Auschwitz.

Milena Jesenská dies a political prisoner in Ravensbrück.

Felice Bauer lived until her death in 1960 in the USA.

In 1968 the eighty-four-year-old Max Brod gives his last interview about his friend Franz Kafka with the journalist Georg Stadtler.

Was he a cheerful person?

That is going a bit far! He was not as depressed as he is made out to be today, but you could not call him a CHEERFUL PERSON, no,

CITATIONS

[Note: all translations are by the current translator]

p. vii: 'Think of me as a dream.' In a 1968 interview Max Brod recalls the scene when Kafka unintentionally woke up Brod's sleeping father. Cit. Max Brod in conversation with Georg Stadtler, TV-Interview, BR-alpha from RetroReihe, ARD-/BR-alpha, 1968.

p. 10:   'I'll tear you apart like a fish!', *Letter to His Father*, written in November 1919.

p. 11:   'Perhaps my situation at that time becomes clearer when I compare it with that of Felix. You treat him similarly, and even employ a particularly terrible method against him, in that when he does something at dinner that in your eyes is unclean, you do not content yourself with saying, as you did to me at that time: "You're an utter pig" but add: "a true Hermann" or "just like your father".' *Letter to His Father*.

All italics in *Letter to His Father*.

p. 12:   All italics in *Letter to His Father*.

p. 15:   'What do I have in common with the Jews? I hardly have anything in common with myself and should stand quite still, satisfied that I can breathe, in a corner.' *Diary*, 8.1.1914.

All italics in *Letter to His Father*.

p. 16   All italics in *Diary*, 2.1.1912.

'with this kind of body', *Diary*, 22.11.1911.

p. 17   'As a little boy, when I couldn't swim yet, I sometimes went to the non-swimming section with my father, who couldn't swim either. Then we'd go sit at the buffet together, naked, each with a sausage and half a litre of beer... Just imagine, the monstrous man with this little scared bundle of bones in his hand, how we undressed for example in the small cabin in the dark, how he pulled me out because I was ashamed, how, supposedly, he would teach me how to swim and so on. And then the beer!' Max Brod, *On Franz Kafka*. All other italics in *Letter to His Father*.

p. 18 'You ruled the world from your armchair. Your opinion was right, every other opinion was crazy, overstated, meschugge, abnormal. Your self-confidence was so great that you didn't have to be consistent, and it never stopped you from being right. You might also have no opinion at all on a matter and, as a result, all the other opinions that were possible at all had to be wrong, without exception.' *Letter to His Father*.

All italics in *Letter to His Father*.

p. 19 'massive letter', letter to Milena Jesenská, 21.6.1920.

'My vanity, my ambition did suffer from the way, which became famous among us, you greeted my books: "Put it on the nightstand!" (most of the time you were playing cards whenever a book arrived)', *Letter to His Father*.

p. 20 'It is true that Mother was boundlessly good to me, but, for me, everything was in relation to you, that is, not a very good one. Mother unconsciously played the role of the driver in the hunt. If in some unlikely case your upbringing could have put me on my own feet by generating defiance, aversion, or even hatred, Mother compensated for that by being good, by reasonable speech (she was the archetype of reason in the confusion of childhood), by intercession', *Letter to His Father*.

'She takes me for a healthy young man', *Diary*, 19.12.1911.

p. 21 'I noticed, of course', *Diary*, 31.12.1911.

p. 22 All italics in *Letter to His Father*.

p. 23 'Youth's meaninglessness', *Diary*, 12.1.1914.

'fear of school', 'Jeder Mensch ist eigentümlich' (Everyone is Peculiar), 1916.

'crying during examinations', Max Brod, *On Franz Kafka*.

p. 24 'Now, school was already a horror in and of itself and, on top of it all, the cook wanted to make it even more difficult for me.' Letter to Milena Jesenská, 21.6.1920.

'as my only path into the future', *Diary*, 2.1.1912.

'earthly weight', *Aphorisms*, 1917/18.

'Of course there are possibilities for me', *Diary*, 12.1.1914.

'Everything immediately gives me pause', *Diary*, 21.7.1913.

'I stand on the end platform of the tram', 'The Passenger', 1913.

From an essay by Kafka at the Assicurazioni-Generali insurance company, 1907/08, cit. Klaus Wagenbach, *Franz Kafka. Bilder aus seinem Leben* (Franz Kafka: Pictures of a Life).

'In the office now', letter to Hedwig Weiler, 8.10.1907.

'I shall jump into my novella', *Diary*, 15.11.1910.

'I want to write, with a constant trembling', *Diary*, 5.11.1911.

'back at the office, in the dregs of misery', letter to Felice Bauer, 25.7.1916.

'the office *is truly hell*, I no longer fear any other', letter to Felice Bauer, 7.4.1913.

'My desk at the office was surely never orderly', letter to Felice Bauer, 3.12.1912.

'a horrible double life', *Diary*, 19.2.1911.

'Time is short', letter to Felice Bauer, 1.11.1912.

'At first glance Kafka was a healthy young man', Max Brod, *On Franz Kafka*.

'Intellectually', Max Brod, *On Franz Kafka*.

'gymnastics naked in front of an open window for ten minutes a day', letter to Felice Bauer, 1.11.1912.

'I admired Franz's swimming and rowing skills', Max Brod, *On Franz Kafka*.

'I work with weights', *Diary*, 18.12.1911.

'Total block', *Diary*, 7.2.1915.

'Whatever I touch comes apart', *Aphorisms*.

'I don't hide from people', *Diary*, 28.7.1914.

'Day before yesterday criticized', *Diary*, 8.3.1912.

'need for pleasure', letter to Felice Bauer, 13/14.3.1913.

The White Slave Girl was a sensationalist Danish film about female slavery. A contemporary Czech critic called it 'A very ordinary piece of cinematographic stupidity, nothing more.' However, Kafka mentions the film to Brod several times; in one letter he writes: 'I went with a woman who looked very much like the slave trader from *The White Slave Girl*.' (25.2.1911).

'Was at the movies. Cried.' *Diary*, 20.11.1913.

'capable of enjoying human relationships', letter to Felice Bauer, 6.11.1913.

pp. 35–6   All quotes in Max Brod, *On Franz Kafka*.

p. 37   'Dear Max, I was under the influence of the Fräulein yesterday when arranging the pieces, it is quite possible that some stupidity, a sequence that was perhaps only secretly funny, came about as a result.' Letter to Max Brod, 14.8.1912.

'There's a worm here somewhere', letter to Kurt Wolff, 4.9.1917.

'improbably small selection', Max Brod, *On Franz Kafka*.

'I have too much respect for the books I know from your publishing house to interfere with suggestions, I only ask that you use the largest font size possible, within those intentions that you have for the book.' Letter to Kurt Wolff, 7.9.1912.

'the ninety-nine pages of the first edition', Max Brod, *On Franz Kafka*.

p. 38   'Agathe is very ugly', letter to Max Brod, August 1907.

p. 39   'Frl. Felice Bauer', *Diary*, 20.8.1912.

'The argumentation in general', *Diary*, 9.3.1914.

p. 40   'my favourite work', letter to Kurt Wolff, 19.8.1916.

'I now sentence you', 'The Judgement', written 22/23.9.1912.

'painstakingly inflated mental-health study', cit. Jürgen Born (ed.), *Franz Kafka. Kritik und Rezeption zu seinen Lebzeiten 1912–1924* (Franz Kafka: Criticism and Reception During His Lifetime 1912–1924).

p. 41   'reasonable', letter to Felice Bauer, 7.10.1916.

'Of all that I have written', 'Testamentarische Verfügung' (Will and Testament), 29.11.1922.

p. 42   'Can you discern any kind of sense in "The Judgement"?', letter to Felice Bauer, 2.6.1913.

'"The Judgement" cannot be explained', letter to Felice Bauer, 10.6.1913.

'for a while', Max Brod, *On Franz Kafka*.

p. 80   Italics and 'Like a dog' in *The Trial*.

           'Early this morning for the first time in a long time', *Diary*, 2.11.1911.

p. 81   Felice Bauer text: unrecorded.

           'Germany has declared war on Russia', *Diary*, 2.8.1914.

p. 82   'There is no discussion as regards my demand', *Diary*, 24.1.1915.

           'Coming together would be nice', letter to Felice Bauer, 5.12.1915.

           'Ultimately, you are indeed a girl', letter to Felice Bauer, 2/3.03.1913.

p. 83   'a formal visit', Max Brod, *On Franz Kafka*.

p. 84   'ten minutes or more', letter to Felice Bauer, 9.9.1917.

p. 85   'Measures against Kafka's illness', Max Brod, *On Franz Kafka*.

           'Dear Max, my illness?', letter to Max Brod, 6.10.1917.

p. 86   'a young girl, hopefully only a little ill', letter to Max Brod, 6.2.1919.

p. 87   'You have, Herr Land Surveyor', *The Castle*, written between January and September 1922.

p. 89   'a vigorous fire, unlike any I have ever seen', letter to Max Brod, beginning of May 1920.

           'we are both married', letter to Milena Jesenská, 21.7.1920.

p. 90   'I can still see how eagerly', Max Brod, *On Franz Kafka*.

           'I do not want (Milena, help me!...)', letter to Milena Jesenská, 31.5.1920.

p. 91   'I am dirty, Milena', letter to Milena Jesenská, 26.8.1920.

           'Perhaps I should tell you a bit more about the evening', letter to Milena Jesenská, 20.7.1920.

p. 92   'And anyway we keep on writing the same thing', letter to Milena Jesenská, 26.7.1920.

           'And these letters are nothing but torture', letter to Milena Jesenská, November 1920.

p. 93   'The Kafka. The Kafka is', Franz Blei, *Das große Bestiarium der modernen Literatur* (The Great Bestiary of Modern Literature).

pp. 94–7   All italics and dialogue in 'A Hunger Artist', completed 23.5.1922.

p. 98   'Walks, nights, days', *Diary*, 12.6.1923.

           'Our world is nothing but', Max Brod, *On Franz Kafka*.

pp. 99–103 All italics and dialogue in 'Josephine, the Singer, or the Mouse People', written between 18.3. and 5.4.1922.

p. 104 'at just the right time', letter to Robert Klopstock, cit. Klaus Wagenbach, *Franz Kafka. Bilder aus seinem Leben*.

'Laryngeal tuberculosis identified', Max Brod, *On Franz Kafka*.

pp. 106–9 All italics and dialogue in ibid.

p. 108 'Have you already tasted this year's wine, doctor?', memo, Franz Kafka, *Das Werk – Die Tagebücher – Die Lettere* (Franz Kafka: The Work – The Diaries – The Letters).

p. 113 'Was he a cheerful person?', Cit. Max Brod in conversation with Georg Stadtler, TV-Interview, BR-alpha froc RetroReihe, ARD-/BR-alpha, 1968.

p. 123 'In every town there's some fool ...', cit. Max Brod in conversation with Georg Stadtler, TV-Interview, BR-alpha from RetroReihe, ARD-/BR-alpha, 1968.

pp. 126–7 'I now have a somewhat "delicate" question', cit. Max Brod in conversation with Georg Stadtler, TV-Interview, BR-alpha from RetroReihe, ARD-/BR-alpha, 1968.

In every town some fool
comes up to me after a lecture
to deliver some abstruse,
utterly unfounded opinion
on Kafka.

BIBLIOGRAPHY

Louis Begley, *Die ungeheuere Welt, die ich im Kopfe habe. Über Franz Kafka* (The Tremendous World I Have Inside My Head: On Franz Kafka), Pantheon Verlag, 2009.

Franz Blei, *Das große Bestiarium der modernen Literatur* (The Great Bestiary of Modern Literature), Ernst Rowohlt Verlag, 1922.

Jürgen Born (ed.), *Franz Kafka. Kritik und Rezeption zu seinen Lebzeiten 1912–1924* (Franz Kafka: Criticism and Reception During His Lifetime 1912–1924), S. Fischer Verlag, 1979.

Karl Brand, 'Die Rückverwandlung des Gregor Samsa' (The Re-Metamorphosis of Gregor Samsa), in *Prager Tagblatt*, 11.6.1916.

Karl Brand, *Vermächtnis eines Jünglings* (A Young Man's Legacy), Verlag Ed. Strache, 1920.

Max Brod, *Über Franz Kafka* (On Franz Kafka), S. Fischer Verlag, 1980.

Elias Canetti, *Der andere Prozeß. Kafkas Lettere an Felice* (The Other Trial: Kafka's Letters to Felice), Reclam Verlag, 1983.

Franz Kafka, *Sämtliche Werke* (Collected Works), ed. Peter Höfle, Suhrkamp Verlag, 2008.

Franz Kafka, *Tagebücher* (Diaries), Vol. 1: *1909–1912*, Vol. 2: *1912–1914*, Vol. 3: *1914–1923*, S. Fischer Verlag, 2008.

Franz Kafka, *Das Werk – Die Tagebücher – Die Lettere* (The Works – The Diaries – The Letters), ed. Max Brod, Verlag Lambert Schneider, 2012.

Andreas B. Kilcher, *Franz Kafka. Leben, Werk, Wirkung* (Franz Kafka: Life, Work, Impact), Suhrkamp Verlag, 2008.

Andreas Kilcher, *Franz Kafka. Die Zeichnungen* (Franz Kafka: The Drawings), C.H. Beck Verlag, 2021.

David Zane Mairowitz/Robert Crumb, *Kafka*, Reprodukt, 2013.

Vladimir Nabokov, *Die Kunst des Lesens. Meisterwerke der europäischen Literatur* (The Art of Reading. Masterpieces of European Literature), S. Fischer Verlag, 1982.

Reiner Stach, *Kafka. Die frühen Jahre* (Kafka: The Early Years), S. Fischer Verlag, 2016.

Reiner Stach, *Kafka. Die Jahre der Entscheidungen* (Kafka: The Decisive Years), S. Fischer Verlag, 2004.

Reiner Stach, *Kafka. Die Jahre der Erkenntnis* (Kafka: The Years of Insight), S. Fischer Verlag, 2010.

Klaus Wagenbach, *Franz Kafka. Bilder aus seinem Leben* (Franz Kafka: Pictures of a Life), Verlag Klaus Wagenbach, 1983.

Klaus Wagenbach, *Franz Kafka*, rororo-Monographie, Rowohlt Verlag, 2008.

Hanns Zischler, *Kafka geht ins Kino* (Kafka Goes to the Movies), Galiani Berlin bei KiWi, 2017.

Special thanks to Radek Knapp for our discussion at Café Hummel, Vienna, on 1st March 2023.

I now have a somewhat delicate question. You knew Kafka personally. For you, as a literary historian, isn't it a bit of a burden to have been such close friends with him, that is, perhaps there is not enough distance for you to interpret Kafka's work?

A distance that others who did not know him personally do have?